A Window into Life on Mingulay

Extracts from the School Log Book 1875-1910

Contributions by

Ben Buxton and David Powell

Edited by

Bob and Shirley Chambers

An Islands Book Trust Publication

The Islands Book Trust

Laxay Hall

Laxay

Isle of Lewis

HS2 9PJ

Tel: 01851 830316

www.theislandsbooktrust.com

Copyright remains with the named authors. Other than brief extracts for the purpose of review, no part of this publication may be reproduced in any form without the written consent of the publisher and copyright owner.

© The Islands Book Trust 2012

ISBN: 978-1-907443-37-4

British Library Cataloguing in Publication Data: A CIP record for this book can be obtained from the British Library.

All rights reserved. No part of this publication may be reproduced, stored in a retrieval system, or transmitted in any other form or by any means, electronic, mechanical, photocopying, recording or otherwise without the prior written permission of the publishers. This book may not be lent, hired out, resold or otherwise disposed of by way of trade in any form of binding or cover other than that in which it is published, without the prior consent of the publishers.

The Islands Book Trust would like to thank Donnie Morrison for help with the production of this volume.

Log Book scanned images© Comhairle nan Eilean Siar

Printed and bound by Pairc Press

Contents

	Page
An introduction to Mingulay by Ben Buxton	6

More than the history of a school: The Mingulay School Log Book in context
by David Powell — 17

Extracts from the Mingulay School Log Book 1875-1910 — 25

Biographies — 43

FOREWORD

This year sees the centenary of the abandonment of Mingulay as a permanent human settlement. The Islands Book Trust are marking the anniversary by a conference about the history of the island; and this publication which contains extracts from the log book of Mingulay school between 1875 and 1910, alongside introductory chapters about the dramatic history of the island and its schools by Ben Buxton and David Powell.

We are also organising a new limited edition of stamps and a postal cover to mark the Mingulay centenary, and the re-lettering of the headstone at Cuithir, Barra, of John Finlayson, the Mingulay teacher who figures prominently in the history of its schools and the log book.

Mingulay deserves to be remembered. It is a beautiful island and was home for centuries to a Gaelic-speaking community with a rich culture of stories and songs. It has sometimes been compared with the better known St Kilda. Certainly, many of the factors which led to population decline and its eventual abandonment are similar, for example the lack of a reliable harbour, so that islanders were regularly cut off from the outside world for lengthy periods during the winter.

I hope that this publication, ably edited by Bob and Shirley Chambers, will serve as a memorial to the people of Mingulay, and indeed offer a window into the daily life of the final years of the community.

John Randall
Chairman
The Islands Book Trust
June 2012

Map of Mingulay (Ordnance Survey)

Ruins in the deserted island of Mingulay as it is today (John Randall)

An Introduction to Mingulay

Ben Buxton

Mingulay is the last but one of a chain of five small islands strung out like jewels at the southern end of the Outer Hebrides. In size 4 kilometres (2 ½ miles) long, it is the second largest of the five islands south of Barra: Vatersay, Sandray, Pabbay, Mingulay and Berneray. Viewed from the sea, however, it appears to be the biggest, and it is also the highest, rising to 273 metres. This may account for the origin of its name: Big Isle in Old Norse.[1]

The islands are part of Barra Parish, described in 1847 as "composed of a cluster of islands surrounded by a boisterous sea, making the passage from one island to another a matter of very considerable hazard." For thousands of years all five southern islands were inhabited, but since 1912, when the last of Mingulay's native population gave up the struggle for survival there, only Vatersay has had a human population.

Mingulay's shape was once likened to a "figure eight written with a shaky pen." The broad eastern indentation, Mingulay Bay, where the landing places are, has a magnificent sandy beach at its head; inland from there, and now partially buried in it, lie the sad remains of the village. Lush green pasture, the former fields of the inhabitants, extends inland into a broad glen enclosed by an amphitheatre of barren hills, rocky and treeless. A small valley, Skipisdale, opens onto the south coast.

On the Atlantic side of the island the hills plunge to the sea in tremendous cliffs, eaten away by the relentless pounding of the ocean. The cliffs are festooned in the breeding season with seabirds, and, together with the cliffs of neighbouring Berneray, support one of the most important seabird colonies in Britain. There are fifteen breeding species, the most numerous being razorbills, guillemots, fulmars, and kittewakes. The islands are together designated a Site of Special Scientific Interest and a Special Protection Area on account of the seabirds and the maritime and paramaritime vegetation.

Mingulay's remoteness, cliffs, seabird populations and (former) isolated human communities are reminiscent of Hirta, the main island of the St Kilda group. Indeed, one Victorian writer called Mingulay "the nearer St Kilda." And there were similarities in the way of life of the inhabitants of the two islands.

Before its isolation became a handicap in the later 19th century, Mingulay was a good place to live. Resources were abundant: fish in the sea, seabirds on the cliffs, grazing for cattle and sheep, fertile soil for crops, and peat for fuel. The sea was a highway rather than the barrier it was to become as people became more dependent on the outside world.

Mingulay's first inhabitants were probably Neolithic farmers around 5,500 years ago. Former inhabitants have left traces scattered all over the island. Arrangements of stones, or piles of stones, can be anything from less than a century old to over 5,000 years old, and very often, stones have been re-used over time. Stones from Iron Age roundhouses have been rebuilt into later structures, in one case as recently as the 1920s, to make a sheep pen. Rectangular stone settings high in the hills have been variously interpreted by archaeologists as a Mingulay variant of a type of Bronze Age burial monument, or as much more recent platforms for stacks of cut peat.

Several round houses of Iron Age date (roughly 400BC to 500AD) show that Mingulay had a substantial population at that time. Two of these are in Skipisdale, and an ancient field system, with stone walls partially buried in peat, may date from this time.

Like its neighbours, Mingulay had a chapel in medieval times. It was situated on a knoll which in recent times, and probably for many centuries, was a burial ground. The chapel, which was last mentioned in the 17th century, may have been built in the 12th century, but it is possible that there was an earlier chapel. Nearby Pabbay has a similar although much more pronounced knoll with cross-incised grave stones dating from between the 6th and 8th centuries, and the island's name means Priests' Isle in Old Norse.

The Hebrides were raided and settled by Vikings from Norway from the end of the 8th century and were part of the Norse Kingdom of the Isles until 1266. The majority of the place names of Mingulay and its neighbours, and of the islands themselves, are Norse. The suffix –ay means island in Old Norse.

Mingulay was inhabited when it was first mentioned in the 16th century. At this time the islands south of Barra were known as the Bishop's Isles, having some sort of connection with the Bishop of the See of the Isles. However, they were part of the territory of the clan MacNeil, and Mingulay people paid rent to the clan chief in produce from the island, including seabirds, mainly young shearwaters.

It might have been at about this time that the legendary plague occurred. The story goes that nothing had been heard of the Mingulay people for a while, so MacNeil of Barra sent a boat to investigate. One of the crew, MacPhee, went ashore and found that all the people had died of plague. When he returned to shout the news to the others, they fled, dreading infection, and MacPhee was left alone. Every day he climbed the hill, later named after him, looking for a boat that would rescue him; eventually he was saved, and was allowed to settle on Mingulay.

In the late 18th century, 52 people, consisting of eight or nine families, were recorded. This was probably a suitable number for the island to support, but in the 1830s the population more than doubled. In about 1834, the inhabitants of the islands south of Barra were evicted by the clan chief, General MacNeil of Barra, and replaced with more profitable sheep. This sort of thing was common in the Hebrides at the time, part of the process known as The Clearances, but MacNeil was excessively brutal. He forced the evicted islanders to work at his kelp (seaweed) works at Northbay, Barra which he had built in a desperate attempt to stave off bankruptcy. Processing kelp produced ingredients used in the manufacture of soap and glass. The enterprise failed, and the MacNeils' ancestral lands were sold off. In about 1837 people returned to the southern islands, with the exception of Sandray, where the sheep remained and the former human inhabitants ended up on Mingulay.

By the time of the first population census of 1841, 114 people (18 households) were living on Mingulay. The population continued to grow, to 150 (34 households) in 1881. These figures are among many records and visitors' accounts which became available in the later 19th century and allow a picture to be built up of life on the island.

Cemetery on Mingulay (John Randall)

The people lived by fishing, catching seabirds on the cliffs, and crofting, that is, raising cattle and sheep and growing a few crops. They had a rich Gaelic culture and were devout Roman Catholics. The Protestant Reformation never took hold in these outposts, and the islands of South Uist and Barra remain Roman Catholic to this day. Mingulay society was egalitarian, and, because of their remoteness, the people enjoyed a certain amount of Home Rule.

The tentacles of the outside world began to penetrate in 1859, when a school was established by the Ladies' Highland Association, also known as the Free Church Ladies' Association (Edinburgh Branch). Hitherto, education in the Barra Isles had been provided sporadically by various religious and philanthropic organisations. For a few years at the end of the 17th century Barra boasted one of only two Catholic schools in Scotland at the time, its main function being to train young men for the priesthood. A century later, the Society in Scotland for the Propagation of Christian Knowledge, founded to counter Catholicism and the Gaelic language, set up a school. Then, in the early 19th century, the Gaelic Schools Society, which taught the reading of the scriptures in Gaelic, provided itinerant teachers in Barra, and, in 1822, in the island of Sandray. By 1860 Barra had four schools: one Catholic, one Church of Scotland (the parish school), and two run by a new organisation, the Ladies' Highland Association.

This Association had been founded in 1850, seven years after the establishment of the Free Church of Scotland by disaffected ministers of the Church of Scotland. The Association had three principal objectives: firstly, to attempt to improve the conditions of the population of the Highlands and Islands after the terrible famines of the 1840s by providing schools (and, in poor districts, clothing to enable children to attend); secondly, to use the schools as a training ground for the young men training for the ministry in the new Church; and thirdly, "to bear upon the popery (Catholicism) which still exists in some Highland districts." Mingulay was the only solidly Catholic island to get a school, and the most remote. The schools were known locally as the "Ladies' Schools" (Sgoil nan Leitidhean). The organisation was funded by private donations; fees were not charged, but local people were expected to contribute to the provision of buildings, and food for the teachers. The Mingulay School features in many of the annual reports of the Association.

Mingulay appears to have got its school largely by accident. In 1857, one of the (Protestant) lighthouse keepers on Barra Head (on Berneray, the island to the south) appealed to the Association for a teacher. He "promised that half the salary would be raised by the people, and that about 70 children would attend", most of who would have come from Mingulay as Berneray's population was much smaller. In early 1859, however,

> "The light keeper, expecting to be relieved, withdrew his offer of aid, and most of the people were in the adjacent island of Mingalay, where nobody could be found to make any preparation for the teacher ... It was felt to be a very perilous and difficult experiment to send a young man to so remote a place where nobody could read, and all were Roman Catholics ... however, a young man being found willing to make the trial, he was sent in May, and was so well received, that in a few weeks he had a flourishing school of about sixty scholars, was lodged by the people as comfortably as they could, and in August, when the barn was required in which the school had been taught, they offered to build a new house if a little aid could be given them for timber for the roof and windows, for which they had to send a boat to Fort William ... the progress the children have made has been very encouraging, and this arduous enterprise has hitherto succeeded beyond the most sanguine expectations."

According to a tradition current in Barra, the teacher, John Finlayson, was destined for Berneray and was taken there by Duncan Sinclair, a crofter there who is known to have been concerned about his children's education, and who would have been among those calling for a teacher. However, on the journey from Barra a storm blew up and they had to seek shelter at Mingulay, where Finlayson saw that there were many more children than in Berneray, so he decided to establish the school there.

End view of Mingulay's first school, sketched by T. S. Muir in 1866.
(The picture was published in T. S. Muir, Barra Head, a Sketch 1867)

Finlayson's early days cannot have been easy: he was the first recorded outsider to live there, and brought with him the values and language of the outside world, and a foreign religion. T. S. Muir, who visited in 1866, speculated on his task:

> "The labour of breaking in even so merely a handful of utterly uncultivated homespuns must have been dreadful. It is supposed that [Finlayson] went forth to the task sufficiently apprised of the material upon which he was to operate; but if not, his earliest encounter with his sucklings-elect must have somewhat suddenly perfected his knowledge. Upon his landing in Mingula, the tiny vagrants crowded round to see the school they had been told they were going to have. They thought he had it with him packed up in his trunk!"

John Finlayson was born in 1830 in Lochcarron, Ross-shire, the son of a tailor who joined the Free Church on its formation. He attended Edinburgh University, but never graduated. His appointment to Mingulay was his first with the Ladies' Highland Association, who must have considered him equal to perhaps their toughest post. He was a shy, scholarly, un-ambitious man - not, one would have thought, the proselytising type - and a conscientious teacher. To the islanders he was known as 'an Sgoilear Glas', the Grey-Haired Teacher.

The school was visited, and the children examined, at intervals by supporters of the Association. The first of these, in 1860, reported that the 33 pupils "showed considerable acquaintance with Scripture, and had made good progress in acquiring English." Three years later 24 children could read the Bible, and could write letters to their teacher when he was at college. Originally the schools were intended to operate for only half the year, as the teacher was expected to spend the winter months at Free Church College in Edinburgh as part of his training for the ministry.

The intelligence and ability of the children impressed the visitors, such as a Mr Ross in 1868: "The Bible lesson was remarkably well read by every one of the 18 who were present ... The examination upon the lesson was conducted in English, and as readily answered in English ... their spelling and translation from English and Gaelic was well done ... the writing was wonderfully good ... a number of them performed sums in the advanced rules of arithmetic." At John Cowan's visit in 1865 there were "17 boys and ten girls; the latter were tolerably well dressed, for our visit was expected. The boys were very quaint in their rags - petticoats or sacks. One piece of dress was thought sufficient for a child, and the feet were all bare."

The first school building was situated on its own on the northern edge of the village, overlooking it. It was, said Muir, "externally in no way distinguished, excepting in length, from the neighbouring huts." In 1865 "there was no glass in the windows and many crevices in the roof through which the sun's rays slanted, helping to lighten up the room." Inside it was "furnished with a few desks and forms" an improvement on 1860 when "writing was performed on a plank or seat, the children kneeling in the sand." The children normally wrote in copy-books, but in 1865 these had not arrived, so roof slates saved from a wreck were used, the children writing with stalks of pipes instead of pencils. At Muir's visit in 1866, one end of the building, separated by a curtain, served as Finlayson's Spartan-living accommodation.

In terms of its educational function, "the teacher and school are highly appreciated by the people", wrote Ross in 1863. But the missionary function of the school must not be forgotten. The 1859 report reads: "The success of this school proving, as it does, that a wide and effectual door is open for diffusing gospel light in all parts of Scotland where Popish darkness still prevails, Christians will surely be stimulated to remove what is indeed a reproach - the fact that there are districts which the Reformation has never reached." Given such attitudes, conflict was inevitable.

In the early years, the Association was content with religious instruction during school hours, but it also wanted attendance at Sunday Schools. This was sensitive in the Catholic islands. The 1864 report says: "The people have been warned that unless attendance is secured on Sabbath as well as week-days the school may not be continued." This threat to close the school was carried out in 1871: "The school in the island of Mingalay ... was found lately in so unsatisfactory a state that the Committee were advised to drop it for a time, perhaps to be resumed at a future period under a new labourer."

This was a thinly-veiled attack on Finlayson and, presumably, his perceived failure to get children to attend Sunday school, or even gain converts, was more to do with the Association's naiveté in thinking conversion could be achieved in such a close-knit Catholic community. Mingulay was not the same as Barra, where there were some Protestants. The criticism of Finlayson may seem unfair, but there may be more to it than the report let on. In November 1871 he married an islander, Jane Campbell, and it is tempting to speculate whether this had anything to do with the school's closure. The marriage to a Catholic would have been unacceptable to the Association, and Finlayson's position would have become impossible.

The wedding took place not long after the closure of the school - if we assume that he was no longer in post at the time of his wedding - for the school was still open in July 1871. The wedding was held, unusually, in Mingulay (most weddings of Mingulay people were held in Barra), and it was a Catholic ceremony. He was then 41, she 45; they had no children, but later brought up a grandniece of hers, Maria Campbell.

John Finlayson spent the rest of his life in this remote Catholic community. In 1875 he was employed as teacher at the new school set up by the Barra School Board, and remained in post until he retired in 1897. Surviving letters show that he was passionate about the wildlife of the island and also loved fishing; they also reveal that he was not sympathetic to the islanders' values and religion. He must have kept these feelings to himself on Mingulay, for in the collective memory of the people of Barra and Vatersay he is remembered with great respect.

Finlayson died in 1904 and his body was taken to Cuithir, Barra, to be buried in the graveyard of the Church of Scotland there. The sea was so stormy that the boatmen, fearing the coffin would be washed overboard, lashed it upright to the mast so that, even in death, it seemed that their teacher stood before them.

The Barra School Board School is described in David Powell's contribution to this volume.

Living conditions both improved and deteriorated in different respects, in the later 19th century. Many islanders improved their houses by moving the open fire from the middle of the floor to fireplaces and chimneys in end walls. They added glazed windows set into the walls, instead of having what were little more than holes at the base of the thatch. More islanders were earning cash in the developing fishing industry.

Despite these improvements, however, conditions were deteriorating. The population rose to over 150 in the 1880s, too high for the island to support, and although more crofts were created, the number of people without crofts (who were known as cottars) increased. Although they and their families would have shared relatives' crofts, this caused hardship and was one of the factors in the desertion of Mingulay. The rising population also led to overcrowding in the village, and there were outbreaks of diseases such as typhoid, measles and influenza. It was often impossible to get to Barra to summon the doctor, or, just as importantly, the priest.

A consequence of the rise in population and pressure on land was the need to supplement income by earning cash, either in the developing fishing industry, or further afield such as in the shipyards and gasworks in Glasgow. Fishing was an important element in the economy of Mingulay. Fishing was by line, for white fish such as cod and ling; the fish were cured on the rocks and the fishermen sold them as far away as Glasgow and Northern Ireland. In 1870 Castlebay, Barra, was developed as a fishing port, mainly for herring, and this gave more opportunities for selling fish and for employment on herring boats, and, for women, as herring gutters. For some islanders, this employment meant working on the east coast of Scotland and even England, following the migrating herring during the summer. This would have opened the islanders' eyes to the living standards and ways of the outside world. Education would also have had this effect, from 1859 when the first school was opened. Education also gave the islanders the ability and confidence to call for improvements to the landing facilities, and eventually, for new land on Vatersay.

The fishermen were handicapped in their ability to get involved in the fishing industry by their isolation and the lack of a sheltered landing place for boats. Mingulay Bay is too broad an indentation to provide much shelter from the swell or wind. People and goods could be landed on rocks on either side of the bay but boats had to be landed on, and launched from, the beach. This was quite an operation, and necessitated wading up to chest height in the water. The beach could be treacherous to anyone who didn't know it: in 1840 the seven-man crew of a boat which had sought refuge from a storm in the bay were drowned trying to land there.

The growing involvement in the fishing industry, (which meant less time for crofting and fowling) and increasing dependence on supplies from Barra made the lack of a landing place or anchorage increasingly serious. A visitor reported the islanders' problems in landing supplies: "it is no unusual occurrence for them to have to throw their bags of meal into the sea and drag them ashore by means of a rope," and maintained that "it is easier to reach America than to get there." In 1896 the islanders sent a petition to the Secretary for Scotland, appealing for help in constructing a "boat-slip with a boat-hauling convenience." The petition, sent via their MP, was signed by all the island's men and concluded with the hope that "your lordship will lend a favourable ear to the cry of a sorely-distressed community."

The following year the Congested Districts Board was established to promote economic development in crofting areas. In 1901 the Board installed a derrick for loading and unloading people, animals and goods into and out of boats. While this may have been useful, it did not address the main problem, the launching and landing of the boats themselves.

In the meantime, the islanders had received a boost to their spiritual well-being by the building of a substantial chapel, dedicated to St Columba, in 1898. The islanders were devout Roman Catholics, and their faith was fundamental to their lives. The Mingulay people had not had a chapel for several centuries, and hitherto services had been held in houses. Now they had a spacious chapel on the upper floor of the building and accommodation on the ground floor for the visiting Barra priest. The chapel and more frequent visits from the priest would have been welcome since the priest was the most important figure in their lives, and their isolation from him in times of need was another hardship for them.

These improvements were no doubt welcome but were not enough; developments elsewhere now began to play a part in the inevitable abandonment of Mingulay. The population of Castlebay, Barra had been steadily rising but very little new land for crofting or house building had been created, so that, as on Mingulay, many people were landless and living in overcrowded and squalid conditions. For years from 1883 they had appealed for land on Vatersay, off the south coast of Barra. At that time Vatersay was run as a single farm, occupied only by the tenant farmer and his workers. It had been crofted before 1850, when the people, including ancestors of some of the Barra cottars, were evicted. The landowner, Lady Gordon Cathcart, consistently turned down the appeals for Vatersay.

In 1886 cottars from Castlebay raided Vatersay for the first time, in other words, occupied land without the owner's permission. Raiding resumed in 1900, when the cottars were emboldened by the success of raids on the farms of Northbay and Eoligarry in Barra. A small part of Eoligarry farm and the whole of Northbay farm were subsequently bought by the Congested Districts Board for crofting – and the remainder of Eoligarry farm purchased by the Board of Agriculture for Scotland (the successor to the Congested Districts Board) in 1919. Raids were repeated in subsequent years. The Mingulay people no doubt followed events with interest. By 1905 the community was in decline: photographs taken then show that some buildings had been abandoned, and an islander wrote "we spend the winter months lonely and dull ... we shall be like prisoners during the bad weather ... I am hoping to leave Mingulay soon." (She did so soon afterwards.)

In July 1906 four Mingulay cottars joined a large number from Castlebay in a raid on Vatersay, and, for the first time, some of the desperate Barra men began to build huts in the vicinity of the farm buildings. In January 1907 Michael Campbell and others from Mingulay moved into a hut they had built, and they were followed by a stream of other Mingulay settlers throughout 1907 and 1908. Sandray was also raided by Mingulay men.

In April 1907 Lady Gordon Cathcart took legal action against 11 raiders, five of whom were from Mingulay, requiring them to leave Vatersay. Needless to say, the raiders stayed put. They conducted a lively correspondence with politicians and others concerned in the case, their PR man being Neil MacPhee of Mingulay. He was a man of remarkable ability; he must have been a star pupil at the Board school, for he wrote astonishingly articulate and eloquent letters in English, a foreign language to him. The *Glasgow Herald* felt it necessary to correct misconceptions about the raiders: "an impression has got abroad that the Barra raider is a fiercely rebellious fellow. As a matter of fact, he is rather phlegmatic. He is surely the mildest mannered person who ever set a country's laws at defiance."

In June 1908 ten of the raiders were summonsed to appear in person before the Court of Session in Edinburgh where they were sentenced to two months imprisonment. The case, highlighting as it did a widespread problem throughout the crofting areas of Scotland, received widespread coverage in the newspapers and was debated in both houses of parliament.

The Congested Districts Board eventually bought Vatersay in 1909 and created 58 crofts in four townships. About a third of the crofts were taken by Mingulay people. This process took some time, however, as not all the Mingulay people wanted to leave their island.

The school on Mingulay remained open until April 1910 when the teacher, Mrs McShane, was transferred to Vatersay. In 1911 the remaining inhabitants were ordered to leave as the island had been let to a grazing tenant, and the last people left in the summer of 1912. Berneray and Pabbay had already been abandoned by this time, in 1910 and 1911 respectively. The last of the Sandray "raiders" left for Vatersay in 1911, and Sandray became part of the grazing for the southern townships of Vatersay. Among the last inhabitants of Mingulay were, ironically, fishermen - some of whom had already officially moved to Vatersay - who based themselves on Mingulay during the summer.

From 1912 until about 2004, Mingulay was used for the grazing of sheep, and the school buildings served as a base for shepherds. The schoolhouse was used as a dwelling between 1929 and 1936, when John Harold Russell owned the island and lived there. The school room was used as a wool store until it burnt down in 1946. The schoolhouse was re-roofed in corrugated iron in 1986. Mingulay, Berneray and Pabbay were bought by the National Trust for Scotland in 2000, and within a few years the sheep were taken off. Nature has reclaimed the islands.

[1] The sources for this chapter are:

Ben Buxton: *Mingulay: An Island and Its People,* Birlinn 1995, and Ben Buxton: *The Vatersay Raiders,* Birlinn 2008.

The only known photo of the Board School buildings intact. (M. F. Shaw)
(Image reproduced with kind permission of National Trust for Scotland)

The schoolroom (roofless) was built in 1881 and the school house was added in 1894
(Ben Buxton)

Mingulay school buildings in 2009 (Ben Buxton)

More than the history of a school: The Mingulay School Log Book in context

David Powell

Like all archive records, the Mingulay school log book is a document of two lives. In its first incarnation its function was purely administrative. It recorded the day to day activities of the school to provide evidence to its superiors as to the school's progress, attendance levels and activities and to provide evidence to Her Majesty's Inspector of Schools during their annual visit.

In its second life as a document retained within an archive, and now through extracts published in this book, it is no longer an active administrative record but instead is a window into a school's history and Mingulay society for readers and researchers.

The purpose of this short article is to set the log book into the historical context in which it was created and to outline key points in the history of the school as documented within its pages. It will also look into the insights the log book gives us into life on Mingulay that, while not part of the formal education of the children who attended the school, are recorded within its pages. Ultimately, the availability of the log book online allows the reader to discover much of interest for themselves not touched upon within this summary.

An educational context

As discussed by Ben Buxton in his contribution to this publication, and in greater depth within his 1995 publication *Mingulay: An Island and Its People*, schooling on Mingulay commenced in 1859 with the establishment of the Ladies' Highland Association School and the appointment of John Finlayson as its teacher.[1] The State had made provision for schools as early as an Act in Privy Council of 1616, later ratified by the Scottish Parliament in its Education Act of 1633, but this only required parishes to maintain schools "where convenient means may be had". From the 18th century, parish schools were supplemented by charity schools such as those provided by the Scottish Society for the Propagation of Christian Knowledge, the Gaelic Schools Society, the Church of Scotland Ladies' Association and the Ladies' Highland Association (also known as the Free Church Ladies' Association). By 1865, the Parish of Barra had its own parish school, a Church of Scotland Ladies' Association school and two others run by the Ladies' Highland Association, including the one on Mingulay.

The Ladies' School on Mingulay was wound-up in around 1871 and for four years no formal schooling was provided. The school's former Protestant teacher, John Finlayson, remained on Mingulay having married a Catholic woman from the island, Jane Campbell.

The Education (Scotland) Act in 1872 saw education passing into state control. All children were to be educated and the state created a mechanism in which this could be provided. The Act established School Boards consisting of members elected every three years. The Boards were responsible for providing and administering the provision of education across their area with funding coming from a parliamentary grant and local rates. In their earliest days, the School Boards identified current educational provision within their geographic area, undertook a census of children of school age, identified the sites where new schools could be built and appointed teaching staff.

Mingulay fell within the control of the Barra School Board. The earliest minutes of the School Board have not survived, but those from 1888 onwards are still preserved and provide a detailed insight into the management of education within Barra and its adjacent islands. By 1888, schools had been established at Northbay, Craigston (the former parish school) and Castlebay and on the island of Mingulay.[2] As well as the school on Mingulay, a sub-school linked to Mingulay operated for a time on the neighbouring island of Berneray. Mention is made of it in passing within the Inspectors' reports copied into the Mingulay log book from 1884. The 1887 report notes the "discontinuance of the sub-school in Bernera is to be regretted" [pg 120].[3]

Mingulay must have been a quick win for the Board with the former Ladies' School site being available as a school and John Finlayson, a certified teacher, being available to teach. The Board school was therefore opened on Mingulay on 9 November 1875 to provide two daily sessions of education for children aged between 5 and 13, the leaving age being increased to 14 in 1901.

The Barra School Board who established the new school consisted predominantly of the clergy of the parish and the estate's Protestant factor. The Protestant bias of the Board along with their appointment of Protestant teachers was a bone of

---

[1] Buxton, Ben. *Mingulay: An Island and Its People* (Edinburgh: Birlinn, 1995), 100

[2] Barra School Board records are held by Tasglann nan Eilean Siar, collection reference IN4/1. For further information visit www.tasglann.org.uk

[3] Page numbers referred to the printed page number of the log book and not the page number of this publication

contention for many of the parents within the islands of Barra and Mingulay where the majority of individuals were Catholic.[4] It wasn't until 1897 that Mingulay received its first Catholic teacher and local appointment, John Johnston, who had been born on Mingulay but raised on Barra.

The elected Board members appointed at least one manager to each of their schools from within their membership and further non-Board members were also appointed where desirable. Mingulay's additional managers during its existence included priests and doctors who would have reason for visiting the island more frequently than other Board members. Visits were supposed to be undertaken regularly to ensure that the School was complying with its legal responsibilities, including checking the school records and registers. HM Inspectors' reports copied into the log book regularly chastise the managers for not visiting regularly enough and there are several examples of the government grant received by the school being cut by one-tenth due to the Board's neglect. John Finlayson himself notes on 15 February 1876, "This locality being a remote Island of the Atlantic our school is seldom visited by the managers or any member of the School Board" [pg 3].

The Board were also responsible for the attendance of children to the school and appointed Compulsory Officers, sometimes known as the "Whipper In", to monitor attendance and visit defaulting parents. While these were appointed for the three schools on Barra itself, John Finlayson was left to undertake this task on Mingulay at no extra remuneration. His log book entry on 2 May 1876 records him undertaking his duties, "Strict enquiry made after the cause of absence of a few boys and notice thereof given to the parents or guardians" [pg 5].

The School Board were not shy of prosecuting defaulting parents and in October 1903 the Board minutes record 33 defaulters being sent for prosecution in the Sheriff Court that would occasionally meet on Barra. However, no Mingulay parents appear to ever have been summoned although the teachers on Mingulay were providing reports to the Board.

Under the Scottish Education Code of 1873, all schools were required to maintain a log book. The Mingulay log book is a stout, hardbound volume measuring 20cm x 26cm x 3cm. The volume was sold for purpose through stationers and it contains two pages giving detailed instructions to the teacher as to what should and should not be recorded along with sample entries.

The purpose of the log book was administrative rather than historical. It was a tool for keeping the managers informed as to progress and as evidence for HM Inspection visits. However, it contains within its pages a history of the school told by its authors: the teachers, the school managers and the visiting Inspectors.

The School building
The first Board school opened in 1875 in the former Ladies' School. William Jolly described it:

> Their old school at Church Bay was one of the small thatched huts of the island. It consisted of a thick wall of rude stones five feet in height, and the low entrance was formed of the door of a ship's cabin, floated in some wreck. The interior was dimly lit by two small windows, and was open to the sloping rafters. The floor was covered by a light-coloured sand from the adjacent shore ... The whole apartment was, however, beautified by various natural gifts from the sea and land. Every crevice had a wild flower inserted

---

[4] Buxton 107

in it, and these united their various hues with pleasing effect, and shed a refreshing odour through the close, little hut. The window sills also were stuck full of coloured shells, while a string of seabirds' eggs hung in a graceful curve from side to side of the room. The seats were formed of ships' planks resting on stones set all round the walls, and the only two desks consisted of flat boards nailed to the uprights driven into the ground.[5]

The log book entry for 17 April 1877 suggests that it moved at this date to a new school room, although this ambiguous entry could possibly refer to a rearrangement of the furniture in the current school room that lifted the children's spirits [pg 18]. The building, however, was not fit for purpose and the Inspector's report entered into the log book on 27 September 1880 reports "This School is taught in a hovel with appliances more in harmony with the premises than with present requirements". The situation was finally remedied on 19 September 1881 when the new purpose-built schoolroom designed by Alexander Ross was opened on a new site to the south of the main village. In his report, the Inspector states: "The new buildings which are occupied for the first time on the day of the examination are well built, fully lighted, and fairly spacious, circumstances which no doubt will affect favourably the general efficiency of the school" [pg 77].

A separate dwelling house attached to the school for the teacher was not provided until 1894, built by the Barra-based contractor Alex Maclean of Borve. The teacher, John Finlayson, presumably took possession of the house in late 1894 as the Board minutes of 4 January 1894 record a letter from him complaining upon "the unsatisfactory condition of his new house arising from a defective chimney vent and other imperfect workmanship".[6]

Sarah McShane outside the school house with her pupils in August 1909. The three children nearest to her are her own. (RMR Milne Album, 1909)

(Image reproduced with kind permission of National Trust for Scotland)

---

[5] Jolly, William. 'The Nearer St Kilda: Impressions of the Island of Minglay', *Good Words* (1883), 716-720
[6] IN4/1/R.334 Barra School Board Minute book 1888-1902

Teaching staff

The log book was supposed to be updated on at least a weekly basis. It was to document the attendance of pupils and staff, reasons for school closure, visits of HM Inspectors and managers and comments on the progress of the children. Separate attendance registers and admission registers were kept that were to be inspected by the managers and HM Inspector.[7]

Over its 35 year history, the school was taught by four individuals. John Finlayson opened the school in 1875, retiring in 1897 having taught several generations of Mingulay children over his 38 years tenure of both the Ladies' and Board schools. He was followed by John Johnston until he was replaced by Miss Margaret Haggarty who resigned in 1903. The final teacher was Mrs Sarah McShane who taught at the school until its closure in 1910. Although the log book entries were not supposed to record their personal opinions, the reader cannot help but gain a flavour of the individuals' character over their period of time in charge of the school from their log book entries. Each teacher starts their tenure with neat and detailed comments of their pupils' progress but these deteriorate in terms of written quality and content over time. The language can seem cruel or shocking to the modern ear describing children as dull or backward but this was not uncommon in the language of the time and the log book was never intended as a public document.

Their entries, coupled with the annual HM Inspection summary copied into the log book, allow us to gain an understanding of the teaching methods and curriculum of the time. Children were arranged into standards, working through set books and the curriculum prescribed by the Scottish Education Department. The core syllabus revolved around the traditional Victorian three "Rs" of reading, writing and arithmetic with some history, geography and singing. In 1878, sewing was added for the girls following a chastisement in the School Inspector's report that these had not commenced yet. John Finlayson's wife, Jane, was appointed as Sewing Mistress with Miss Glancy serving from 1889 to 1890, Miss Mary Campbell from 1890 to 1893 and Miss Maria Campbell from 1894. Navigation lessons were introduced later for the boys along with classes in art and map drawing.

Mingulay was a Gaelic-speaking community but no Gaelic provision was included within the 1872 Education Act. Teaching materials and the syllabus were all English and it was expected by the establishment that English would be the first language of the school room. Early in the log book on 29 February 1876, Finlayson opines, "In some Highland districts, where Gaelic is the mother tongue the correct pronunciation of the English is very badly articulated from the idiom of the one being different from the other such is our experience in this remote Highland locality" [pg 3]. All of the teachers regularly comment on the problems of teaching an English syllabus on the island and the barrier to learning that this presented. This was an issue acknowledged by the HM Inspectors although contradictory advice was often given. The Inspector's report of 2 December 1879 states "Gaelic should be less used especially in the higher classes, the matter should be better known" [pg 54]. Yet the Inspection report of 15 December 1881 states "The teacher should make a liberal use of his Gaelic in imparting an intelligent knowledge of the meanings and matter of the lessons and the practice of bilingual instruction should be a marked feature of the work" [pg 77]. The report of 1887 notes "the native language is judiciously and successfully used to promote an intelligent comprehension of English" and goes on to state that "Gaelic was presented for the first time as a specific language and with very commendable results" [pg 111].

The inspection reports could be stingingly critical and it cannot have been pleasant for the teachers to have copied them into the log book. There are numerous

---

[7] The Mingulay School Admission Register for 1881-1894 survives and is held by Barra & Vatersay Historical Society, Castlebay

examples of a criticism in one report being improved for the next report only for the Inspector to then criticise something else. In the case of the pupil teacher John Johnston who took over the school in 1897 the Inspector provides detailed notes on ways in which subjects should be taught and even criticises his handwriting on the blackboard [pp 183, 194]. Good reports were important for both the teacher and the School Board. Bad reports could see the government grant being reduced and this is seen in reports throughout the log book where deficiencies in history, geography, drill and discipline are punished by a reduction, or nil allocation, of part of the grant. Certainly during Finlayson's time at the school, the teacher received half of the government grant on top of the salary provided by the Board so it was in their interests to maintain a good standard and the cash-strapped Board were obviously reluctant to lose any income.

The Inspectors were not completely dispassionate though and commendation is seen including a note in the report of 1897 remarking upon John Finlayson's "long career of faithful service" following his retirement [pg 177]. An Inspector's role though is to ensure standards within the schools he visits and in 1901 his report on John Johnston's abilities is blunt: "Mr Johnstone [sic] under proper direction, would, no doubt, give satisfaction as a teacher, but in this remote island, with other claims on his attention, the difficulties of his task are too much for him ... The services of a female teacher should be secured". John Johnston was a frequent visitor to Castlebay on weekends and was often stormbound there which he himself records in the log book during his tenure. He made up for these missed days by opening the school on a Saturday.

A female teacher, Miss Margaret Haggarty, was recruited from Liverpool to replace Johnston who was transferred back to Castlebay School. Haggarty's entries appear to show her as a conscientious and diligent teacher of the curriculum but the Inspection report of 1903 points out that "By attempting too much, little may be effectively done" [pg 222]. In August 1903 Margaret Haggarty tendered her resignation, although the School Board had made efforts to encourage her to stay on having failed to recruit a replacement. The Board minute of 14 August 1903 records how they agreed to offer her a £10 salary increase if she would stay.[8] She declined the offer and left the school on 31 December 1903.

Her replacement, Mrs Sarah McShane, took up her position on 18 January 1904. Her lengthy entries in the log book in her first year demonstrate much about her teaching methods and she received positive reports from the Inspector. The School Board minutes of 11 May 1904 record that her husband, Edward McShane, was appointed as the school cleaner and to carry out "trifling repairs". In the same minute they also provided furniture requested for the teacher's dwelling.

The Board minute of 6 February 1905 records the resignation of Sarah McShane as teacher of the school. The School Board advertised for a replacement teacher but no applications were received. A salary increase was therefore offered of £10 for her to remain in post to which she agreed "on condition that she be provided with a suitable bed and bedding and the proportionate part of the increase in her salary be included in the present payment". The Board agreed. She was a formidable woman and not scared to take on authority and attempt negotiation, including writing to the Secretary for Scotland to try and secure a croft on Vatersay when she got nowhere with local officials.[9] Sarah remained at the school until its closure in 1910 during which time she gave birth to several children of her own, although no mention of this comes through in her log book entries. On the closure of the school she transferred to the new school on Vatersay to be reunited with many of her former pupils who had already left Mingulay.

[8] IN4/1/R.335 Barra School Board Minute book 1903-1918
[9] Buxton, 114

A window into a wider world

As well as being a record of the school's history, the log book also gives an insight into island life on Mingulay.

Poor or intermittent attendance was an ongoing issue during all the teachers' tenures at the school and failure to maintain attendance at adequate levels could result in the government grant being reduced. Reasons for absence had to be recorded in the log book. By far the most common reasons for absence give an insight into the religious and crofting life of the island and the island's extreme weather.

A devoutly Roman Catholic Island, feast days of the church were observed resulting in a day's missed school "for children of that persuasion" as the Protestant Finlayson recorded in his entry of 21 June 1878 [pg 33]. Whether this absenteeism on religious grounds truly bothered Finlayson or whether he was recording it for the benefit of the School Inspector is unclear, but it is hard not to hear frustration in his entries of 25 June 1886, "No school on Thursday, being a Roman festival" followed the next week on 2 July "Another Roman Catholic festival prevented a meeting of the school on Tuesday" [pg 108].

The crofting year impinged upon pupil attendance as they were often required to stay at home to help with tasks. This was an issue that plagued all the teachers and all comment on it as it often severely affected attendance for weeks at a time, especially in the spring and at harvest. The reader will find numerous reasons for absence ranging from helping with the peats, laying or picking potatoes, gathering sea-ware (seaweed) [pg 46] and even sheep dipping [pg 247].

The weather was also a hindrance to school openings. Winter months were particularly bad, the school often being closed or the school day being cut short due to snow, strong winds or heavy rain. The teachers diligently noted the reasons for closure. Severe rain or cold would often keep the younger children away.

The remote and hostile environment is most notable within the log book during times of illness and epidemic. Johnston had to deal with several epidemics during his period at the school. An outbreak of measles is recorded in January 1898 that closed the school for four months. The school reopened after "the houses were fumigated and the clothes washed with disinfectant" [pg 181]. In October 1899, a mumps epidemic is reported on the island and in February 1900 an influenza epidemic is "raging in the island" [pg 192]. Johnston himself fell ill with pleurisy at the end of the same month. In the same entry on 23 February, Johnston reports "owing to the severe weather which prevails no boat has left the island for Castlebay, but I expect to go to Castlebay myself to inform the doctor of the prevailing epidemic of influenza" [pg 192].

Margaret Haggarty faced an outbreak of scarlatina in October 1902 [pg 210]. She sent children home but was not aware of a boat leaving for Castlebay that would have allowed her to notify the School Board and doctor. She records in the log book, "No one, from whom to ask advice". At times like this, it must have been a lonely and difficult existence for teachers on the remote islands.

Some illnesses keeping children away were less severe but by no means less painful. Sarah McShane reports children failing to attend due to sore feet on 27 September 1907, a reminder that the children often went barefoot and in unsuitable clothing for the prevailing weather [pg 275].

The final three years of the log book are an important record of the decline in population of the island. From 1907, regular reports of children leaving the school for Vatersay or Barra document the gradual evacuation of the island. Although some children return, briefly, she notes on 23 July 1909 "Children try hard but school is composed chiefly of one family … and although teacher and taught exert all they can, still progress does not satisfy the teacher. The other four scholars do well … " [pg 298].

On 18 March 1910 with a school roll of just nine, Sarah McShane records in the log book "the intention of the Board to discontinue this school, after 30 April 1910" [pg 307]. In March and April the school rooms are overhauled and tidied and the last attendance is recorded as 27 April 1910, closing a few days earlier than intended due to the teacher being ill.

Extracts from the Mingulay School Log Book 1875-1910

Introduction

The following representative sample extracts taken from the log book give a flavour of the entries made over the 35 year life of the school. They cover a surprisingly wide range of topics including school inspections, premises, attendance, curriculum, attainment, teachers, health, weather, religion, croft work, and declining population.

Errors and accidents

The teachers were not infallible and several errors relating to dates appear within the log book's pages. The context of the error is usually obvious. HM Inspectors' reports tend to appear in the log book a few months after the inspection actually took place and readers should check carefully if the date given is the date of entry or the date of inspection.

Pages 280-281 were accidentally missed by Sarah McShane when completing the log book in 1907. On completion of the final page of the log book, she returned to these missed pages where the final entries for 1910 are entered, resulting in the chronology of the log book being slightly out of sequence.

The images presented in this volume are slightly reduced in size from the original. The log book is also freely available online as a digital flip-book at http://www.cne-siar.gov.uk/archives/collections.asp where it is possible to expand the size of the images.

The digitisation of the log book was undertaken in 2011 by the National Records of Scotland through a partnership with Tasglann nan Eilean Siar (Hebridean Archives). The Tasglann project is a three-year project funded by the European Regional Development Fund, *Comhairle nan Eilean Siar* and *Comunn na Gàidhlig* to map the location of archives across the islands and open up access to these records. Further details on the project can be found at www.tasglann.org.uk

The Mingulay log book is physically held by Comhairle nan Eilean Siar and can be accessed by the public at Castlebay Library on Barra. Castlebay Library also holds the log books for the Barra schools at Castlebay (1882-1990), Grean (1910-63), Northbay (1882-1960) and Vatersay (1910-94). *Comunn Eachdraidh Bharraidh agus Bhatarsaidh* (Barra Historical Society) hold the school log books for Craigston (1898-2002).

Teachers of Mingulay School

John Finlayson	1875-1897
John Johnston	1897-1901
Miss Margaret Haggarty	1901-1903
Mrs Sarah McShane	1904-1910

Sewing mistresses

Mrs Jane Finlayson	1878-?1889
Miss Kate Glancy	1889-1890
Miss Mary Campbell	1890-1893
Miss Maria Campbell	1894-?

THE

SCHOOL LOG BOOK,

Mingulay School

EDINBURGH: R. M. CAMERON,
PUBLISHER OF SCHOOL BOARD BOOKS AND FORMS.

INSTRUCTIONS FOR KEEPING LOG BOOK.

Extracted from the New Scottish Education Code, May 1873.

Art. 34. "In every School receiving Annual Grants, the Managers must provide, out of the School Funds, besides Registers of Attendance,—

    (a) A Diary or Log Book.

    (b) A Portfolio to contain Official Letters, which should be numbered in the order of their receipt.

„ **35.** "The Diary or Log Book must be stoutly bound, and contain not less than 500 ruled pages.

„ **36.** "The Principal Teacher must make at least once a week in the Log Book an entry which will specify Ordinary Progress, and other facts concerning the School or its Teachers, such as the Dates of Withdrawals, Commencements of Duty, Cautions, Illness, &c., which may require to be referred to at a future time, or may otherwise deserve to be recorded.

„ **37.** "No reflections or opinions of a general character are to be entered in the Log Book.

„ **38.** "No Entry once made in the Log Book may be removed or altered otherwise than by a subsequent Entry.

„ **39.** "The summary of the Inspector's Report, and any remarks made upon it by the Department, when communicated by the Managers, must be copied *verbatim* into the Log Book, with the names and standing *(Certificated Teacher of the ——— Class, or Pupil Teacher of the —— year, or Assistant Teacher)* of all Teachers to be continued on, or added to, or withdrawn from, the School Staff, according to the decision of the Department upon the Inspector's Report. The Correspondent of the Managers must sign this Entry, which settles the School Staff for the year.

„ **40.** "The Inspector will call for the Log Book at every visit, and will report whether it appears to have been properly kept. He will specially refer to the Entry made pursuant to Article 39, and will require to see Entries accounting for any subsequent change in the School Staff. He will also note in the Log Book every Visit of Surprise (Art. 12), making an Entry of such particulars as require the attention of the Managers."

SPECIMENS OF SUCH WEEKLY ENTRIES.

As have been approved by H. M. Inspectors.

March 21. School opened on Monday morning with praise and prayer. The Rev. Mr Milne, and Messrs Thomson, Arnott and Brown, School Board Members, were present to introduce as Head Teacher to the School, Mr Andrew Brodie, Certificated Second Class, from Free St Peter's Schools, Edinburgh, employed seven years in teaching. The most of the week has been occupied in understanding the arrangement of Classes, &c. Attendance fair. School opened and closed with prayer at the usual hours.

March 28. Attendance irregular this week, chiefly owing to bad weather. On Wednesday afternoon the II. and III. Standards had special drill in Arithmetic. Other Lessons according to Time Tables. Ordinary progress made.

April 4. Easter Week. Holidays.

April 11. Charles Ross, Pupil Teacher, absent on Thursday from sickness. A Monitor employed in his place. Commenced the Shorter Catechism in the Fourth Class this week. Lessons according to Time Tables. School opened and closed with prayer at the usual hours.

April 18. Attendance much better this week. Extra drill has been given this week in preparing for the Government Examination. Progress good. Visit from Mr Duff of the School Board on Friday afternoon, who waited until dismission. Nothing else worthy of remark.

SUGGESTIONS WORTHY OF NOTE.

The yearly date should be at the top of each page. The Log Book must be kept *in* School. One or two lines should be left as a space between each Entry. No special rule can be given as to the length of Entries, but three average Weekly Entries on a page have been accepted in England by Her Majesty's Inspectors. Personal opinions or reflections, such as " unpleasant visit from ———, who gave me much impertinence," are not permitted, and may cause forfeiture of Certificate. Epidemics, fairs, &c., having influence in the attendance,—and new subjects or Books introduced should be noted.

Managers would do well to observe particularly Art. 17, *e*, of Scottish Code, which runs as follows :—" Notice " should be immediately given to the Department of the date at which the Teacher enters on the charge of the " School, from which date the Grant is computed." By inattention to this the whole Grant, or portions thereof, have been frequently forfeited.

Novbr 9th	18 uy5

November 16	This is a new school. The children 30 in number, are all beginners—not one of them knowing the Alphabet. I find all the children quite willing to learn

First entry in School log book 16th November 1875 (p.1)

February 15	This locality being a remote Island of the Atlantic our school is seldom visit ed by the managers or any member of the School Board.

Visit by manager 15th February 1876 (p.3)

February 29	In some Highland districts, where Gaelic is the mother tongue, the correct pronuncia tion of the English is very badly articulated, from the idiom of the one being different from the other. Such is our experience in this remote Highland locality.

Gaelic 29th February 1876 (p.3)

March 28	This week, we had a visit from the Revd J. McDonald of the School Board He remained with us while going through the ordinary work of the day, and ex pressed great astonishment at the progress made by children, placed under so many disadvantages and whose average ex perience of school life does not exceed 180 attendances, the school having been opened for the first time on the 9th of November 1875

Visit of the School Board 28th March 1876 (p.4)

May 2	Good progress is made by the First & Second Classes, Attendance more regular Strict inquiry made after the cause of absence of a few boys and notice thereof given to parents or guardians

Teacher looks into absences 2nd May 1876 (p.5)

November 7	It is just about a year since the opening of this school, it being opened on the 9th November 1875. The progress made since that time is very encouraging In July last we had two classes examined. the one on Standard II the other on the First.

One year progress report 7th November 1876 (p.11)

December 5	The population in this locality being entirely Roman Catholics. a holiday occurred on Thursday so that the number of schools during this week, is, eight.

Church holiday 5th December 1876 (p.13)

April 17	A change of school-room on this week seems to make the children more cheerful and keener to learn, A change for the better is expected as a consequence. Attendance very regular Progress ordinary

Change of school room 17th April 1877 (p.18)

June 21 — Attendance during past week quite
unsatisfactory
Those attending with regularity make
good progress six attendances only on
Thursday, it being a Roman Catholic festival
none of the children of that persuasion put
in an appearance.

Attendance and church holiday 21st June 1878 (p.33)

41

1878   Summary of the Inspectors report

October 21   This school was examined for the first time on
the Island, It is taught with good ability and
very creditable results. Children tidy and very
earnest and smart. The ~~tone was very good~~
and pleasant. The work was ready and very
accurate. Reading very fluent from all, distinct
from many. Meaning very creditable
Grammar good Dictation very good.
Writing good on slate, fair on copy, but
creditable considering the accommodation.
Arithmetic very good. Sewing should
have been taught during last year
and should be begun at once

C. McLellan's name has been struck off
the Examination paper under article 19 (B).

Mr. Finlayson will shortly receive a certificate under article 59.

First school inspection recorded in log book 21st October 1878 (p.41)

June 6	No school on either Thursday or Friday. Attendance still irregular on account of gathering sea-ware, nothing to mention of any importance

Croft work 6th June 1879 (p.46)

54

1880

| December 2nd 1879 | Summary of the Inspector's Report on this School

This school continues to be taught in the same miserable premises, with very great care and geniality, and very creditable work. Order and tone very good, pupils tidy and earnest. Class drill requires more practice. Reading very fluent—except in some of the second standard, but monotonous. Meaning backward throughout. Gaelic should be less used, especially in the higher classes; the matter should be better known. Grammar moderate in the second standard; pretty good in rest. Dictation good in the third standard, pretty good in rest. Writing fair on slate, very creditable on copy. Arithmetic very good in lower standards, fair in higher. History and Geography little known. |
|---|---|

Inspection reports miserable premises and comments on Gaelic recorded in log book 2nd December 1880 (p.54)

77

1881

November 11th — Summary of the Inspectors Report on the School

In many respects, the work in this remote school is very commendable in the circumstances. The new buildings which are occupied for the first time on the day of Examination are well built, fully lighted, and fairly spacious, circumstances which will no doubt affect favourably the general efficiency of the School. Additional forms

?!

blinds and a ball frame should be provided. The present supply of maps is quite inadequate and must be at once increased by the addition of at least a large map of the world and maps of England and Ireland. Reading is too rapid and monotonous and hand-writing should be more distinct and better formed. The Teacher should make a liberal use of his Gaelic in imparting an intelligent knowledge of the meanings and matters of the lessons and the practice of bi-lingual instruction should be a marked feature of the work. Owing to an alleged unacquaintance on the part of the Teacher with the

Inspection Report, new school and use of Gaelic recorded in log book 11th November 1881 (p.77)

Gaelic was presented for the first time as a specific subject and with very commendable results.

Another reference to Gaelic in March 1887 Inspection (p.111)

120

1888

schedule

The discontinuance of the sub school in Bernera is to be regretted J.E.R

John Finlayson. teacher of the third class.

Sub School closing recorded February 1888 (p.120)

April 1st

8th

The presence of Hooping Cough lowered our average attendance in past week, Our average attendance in past month is pretty high. Hooping Cough confined to one house, three pupils are then absent

Reference to whooping cough 1st and 8th April 1892 (p.143)

20

27th

7 pupils withdrawn on account of sore hands. All the other pupils came back on Wednesday. These fell back sadly during their absence 7 pupils are still absent this is a great back

Absences due to sore hands 20th March 1896 (p.167)

1897

4/8/97

Barra, Minglay Public School,
Inverness.

"The results brought out by this
examination, which brings to a close
a long career of faithful service
on the part of Mr. Finlayson are on
the whole very creditable. As usual
Arithmetic is well taught, but
handwriting is still backward in
many respects. Satisfactory attainments
are shown in the other subjects.
Discipline is kindly, but the higher
grant cannot be allowed on account
of the absence of drill"
(Ind.) J.S.R.

John Finlayson retires recorded in log book 4th August 1897 (p.177)

May 31

Notes for the teacher

St I Broaden the letters man not mmm (too sharp & narrow)

St II In this St and in St I get up an addition table. 5+2 5+3 5+5 7+6 8+7 9+8 etc by heart.

be careful with figures 5 not 3, 3 not 5

Teach Geography mainly from the Map.

Use the Blackboard frequently, especially in Grammar and Arith Composition

never talk Gaelic except when absolutely necessary for explanation

Graphic Readers for Sts I & II

Royal Crown Readers for III, IV or V.

Dad

Mr Johnston's school inspection recorded in log book 31st May 1898 (p.183)

" 23rd. — School closed on Medical Authority. Measles fast spreading in the island.

Measles outbreak 23rd January 1898 (p.180)

Oct 28 — I visited this School on the above date & examined the register which I found to be correct. The attendance is not at all very satisfactory & the reason given is an epidemic of mumps. The premises are well & kept.

Mumps outbreak 28th October 1899 (p.191)

" 9th — Influenza raging in the island, Attendance very irregular. Teacher laid up on Thursday with it.

Influenza outbreak 9th February 1900 (p.192)

Mr. Johnstone, under proper direction would, no doubt, give satisfaction as a teacher, but in this remote island, with other claims on his attention, the difficulties of his task are too much for him. He teaches Physical Drill well, and succeeds best in instructing the older pupils of the school, especially one clever boy of sixteen.

Mr. Johnston's Inspection report recorded in log book November 1901 (p.201)

Wk. ending
Oct. 10th

Fresh cases of sickness this week. which is much more serious. there was thought at first. being a mild form. of scarletina.

Outbreak of Scarletina 10th October 1902 (p.210)

Wk. ending
March 6th

Finlay Mackinnon left this school Nov. 7th, went to reside in Castlebay. & attended school there, for a fortnight. He returned to Mingley. 4 months later, and was re-admitted on the 7th of March. Twenty six on Reg. Average 23.

Pupil re-admitted after return from Castlebay 6th March 1903 (p.216)

"By attempting too much" little may be effectively done.

Miss Haggarty's abilities 14th August 1903 (p.222)

Wk. ending
Dec. 31st

Margaret Haggarty resigns charge of Mingley School. this day Dec. 31. 1903

Miss Haggarty resigns 31st December 1903 (p.227)

1904
Jan 18

"I. Mrs S. McShane take charge of this school today. January 18th 1904

Mrs McShane starts 18th January 1904 (p.227)

> Jan 22 "I find school much behind. (See record book for notes.) Commenced Tonic Solfa for the first time. Grammar entirely unknown. Consequently the composition is very weak. Commenced to teach the various parts of a sentence Arithmetic also much behind. Discipline is weak. Children seem bright and active enough if firmly handled." — Attendance excellent.

New teacher's comments 22nd January 1904 (p.228)

> Feb 12th Received usual dole of coals. Gave demonstration lessons on writing from blackboard to whole school simultaneously. Continued fractions, taught & subtraction of. Attendance fairly good considering the coldness of the school and severity of the weather. Received about two cwts? coal for use of this cold school.

Record of lessons and receipt of coals for cold school 12th February 1904 (p.229)

> April 1st Perfect attendance all week. Children much improved in all stages of their work. Unfortunately however I can't record anything like perfection yet.

Attendance and standard of work 1st April 1904 (p.231)

October 4th   Summary of H. M. I's Report
     on the School. 20/9/04

The new teacher has made
a promising start.
The pupils are creditably
intelligent, and, in the special
circumstances, the efficiency
of the work may be regarded
as quite satisfactory.
Improvement in certain
subjects indicated to the teacher
will be looked for next year.

     Grant £46. 14. 9.
     Sarah McShane
     Art 79.

William MacMaster.
Dec 19th /04

Mrs. McShane's first inspection recorded in log book 4th October 1904 (p.236)

September 1st   Attendance on ~~Tuesday~~
Monday very poor. Children
staying away to assist in
the process of Sheep —
dipping. Attendance on
other days good. Usual
school work gone through

Reference to sheep dipping 1st September 1905 (p.247)

August 10th — Splendid attendance all week. School visited on 9th Inst by Rev W MacKenzie Member of the School Board. Four hours day on Friday on account of heavy rain and thunder storm. Received school materials on Thursday for current year.

Reference to minister's visit, weather and materials 10th August 1906 (p.260)

August 31st — Splendid attendance all week. Good progress in all work. Girls received needle work materials for current year. One girl received prize of 5/- from teacher for regular attendance, not having missed once for a whole year.

Prize for full attendance 31st August 1906 (p.261)

September 7th — Attendance on Monday & Tuesday only fair. Children absent peat-gathering.

Peat gathering 7th September 1906 (p.261)

October 12th — Girls attendance poor. Kept at home to assist in potato-lifting. Stormy weather prevalent. Usual school routine strictly followed. School very cold.

Girls at home potato lifting, school very cold 12th October 1906 (p.263)

Nov 23
. 30

School closed for two weeks on account of teacher's illness.

School closed due to teacher's illness 23rd and 30th November 1906 (p.265)

Dec 28th

Very stormy weather prevented any meeting of school on Thursday afternoon or Friday. Attendance poor on other days of week. No firing for school. Prevailed on children to fetch peats. Number of scholars present too few to provide adequate number of peats to make a one good fire.

References to weather, heating and peats 28th December 1906 (p.266)

Sept 27th

Boys attendance poor this week. Some suffering from sore feet.

Reference to sore feet 27th September 1907 (p.275)

July 23rd

Attendance good. Children try hard, but school is composed chiefly of one family who are naturally very dull, and although teacher and taught, exert all they can, still progress does not satisfy teacher. The other four scholars do well, but the dull ones are a great hinderance.

Falling numbers mentioned on 23rd July 1909 (p.298)

10/8/09

Received from Clerk to day copy of Schedule of grants for Barra, Mingulay School. Dated July 30th '09

Grants amounting to £26.5.9 have been allowed as set forth in the accompanying Schedule, and payment will be made in course of a few days
Gross total of claim
£26.5.9.
No examination took place.

S. McShane
Teacher
10/8/09

Grant to the school 10th August 1909 (p.299)

March 18th
Return to Page 280.

One boy re admitted on Monday. No on roll 9. Received intimation from Clerk on 15th Inst of the intention of Board to discontinue this school, after the 30th April 1910.

End of the school announced on 18th March 1910 (p.307)

April 27th

Last attendance in this school completed today, Teacher being taken ill at 11 p.m. on above date, hence school closes prematurely.

21/6/10 J.McS

Last entry in the log book 27th April 1910 (p.281)

Biographies of contributors

Ben Buxton got to know Mingulay during a five-week stay in 1975. In 1980 he carried out an archaeological survey for his BA in archaeology at Durham University. He continued research into the history of the island and its neighbours, and in 1995 *Mingulay: An Island and Its People* was published by Birlinn. It was awarded the 1997 Michaelis-Jena Ratcliffe Prize for Folklife. *The Vatersay Raiders* followed in 2008, the centenary of the court case which made the raiders famous. The book is also a history of the island before the raiders. He is currently working as Project Officer on a community heritage project in Sandford, Dorset.

David Powell qualified as an archivist from the University of Liverpool in 2001 having previously undertaken a music degree. Since then, he has spent his professional life working as an archivist in Scotland in the university and local government sectors. This has seen him doing everything from cataloguing the archives of businesses and organisations through to running training courses for community archives, co-authoring the National Strategy for Business Archives and teaching on both of Scotland's Archive Master's degree courses. Since 2010, David Powell has been Project Manager & Archivist with Tasglann nan Eilean Siar (Hebridean Archives), a three-year project funded by the European Regional Development Fund, Comhairle nan Eilean Siar and Comunn na Gàidhlig. The project is mapping archival resources located across the Western Isles held by businesses, organisations, individuals and the voluntary heritage sector in order to allow the archive collections of the islands to be seen as a distributed whole. As well as working closely with archive custodians and historical societies, the Tasglann team care for and make accessible the archives of Comhairle nan Eilean Siar and its predecessor authorities, and this includes the Mingulay log book. To find out more, please visit www.tasglann.org.uk.

THE ISLANDS BOOK TRUST

– high quality books on island themes in English and Gaelic

Based in Lewis, The Islands Book Trust are a charity committed to furthering understanding and appreciation of the history of Scottish islands in their wider Celtic and Nordic context. We do this through publishing books, organising talks and conferences, visits , radio broadcasts, research and education on island themes. For details of membership of The Islands Book Trust, which will keep you in touch with all our publications and other activities, see www.theislandsbooktrust.com

or phone 01851 830316.

The Islands Book Trust, Laxay Hall, Laxay, Isle of Lewis, HS2 9PJ
(01851 830316)